This
Nature Storybook
belongs to:

_____

_____

For Brian G. M.J.

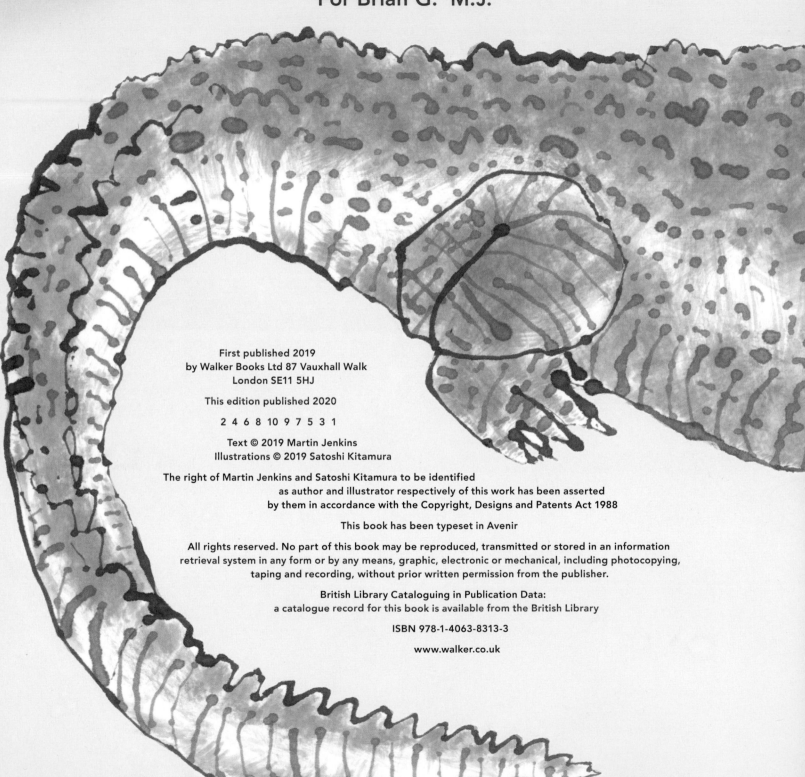

First published 2019
by Walker Books Ltd 87 Vauxhall Walk
London SE11 5HJ

This edition published 2020

2 4 6 8 10 9 7 5 3 1

Text © 2019 Martin Jenkins
Illustrations © 2019 Satoshi Kitamura

This book has been typeset in Avenir

British Library Cataloguing in Publication Data:
a catalogue record for this book is available from the British Library

ISBN 978-1-4063-8313-3

www.walker.co.uk

BEWARE OF THE CROCODILE

Pictures by
MARTIN JENKINS SATOSHI KITAMURA

WALKER BOOKS
AND SUBSIDIARIES
LONDON • BOSTON • SYDNEY • AUCKLAND

The main thing about crocodiles is they're really scary –

or at least the big ones are. They've got an awful lot of ...

teeth.

And they're not at all fussy about what they eat,
as long as it's got a bit of meat on it.

And when it comes to hunting down their dinner,
they're very determined and very cunning.
They know all the spots along the sides of the rivers
and lakes where animals come down to drink.

When it's time for a meal, a hungry crocodile
will choose one of the spots and hide there
in the water, just under the surface, with only
the top of its head sticking out.

Sooner or later, something passing by,
something with a bit of meat on it,
will decide that it's thirsty and needs a drink.
And then?

Then there'll be a sudden **lunge** and a tremendous

SPLASH

And then?

Oh dear.

What happens next is rather gruesome.

In fact it's so gruesome I decided to skip the details.

Let's just say there's a lot of **twirling** and **thrashing**,

then things all go a bit quiet.

Afterwards, the crocodile won't need to feed again for a while. Instead it spends its time cruising around, checking out places where it might find its next meal, or snoozing on a sandbank.

Crocodiles can go for weeks and weeks without eating. The bigger a crocodile's meal, the longer it can go before the next one.

But there's more to crocodiles than SPLASH, snap, twirl, swallow.

You might be surprised to hear that they make very good parents.

Or mothers, I should say. (We'll get on to the fathers later.)

When she's ready to lay some eggs, a mother crocodile gathers up a huge mound of rotting leaves.

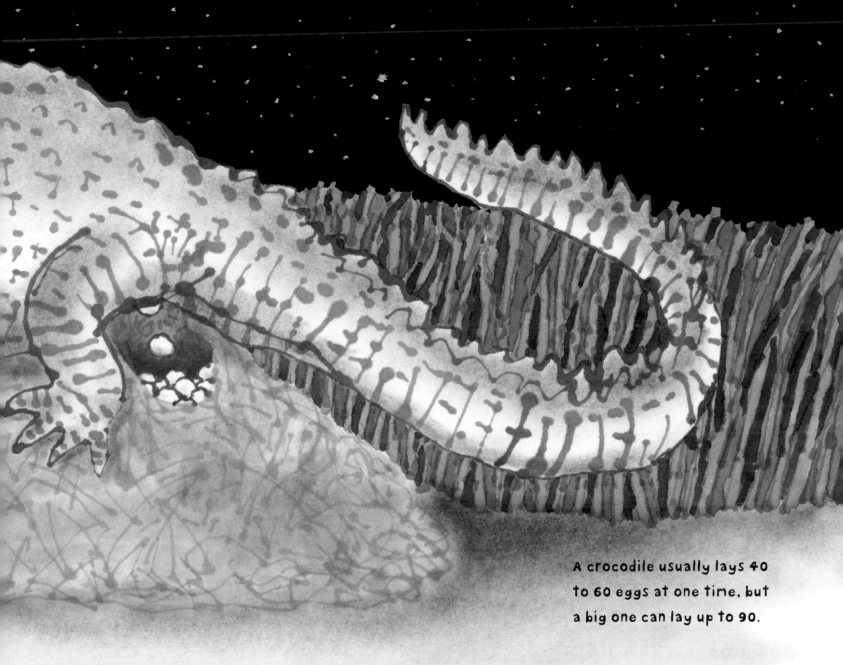

A crocodile usually lays 40 to 60 eggs at one time, but a big one can lay up to 90.

She scoops out a hollow in the top, lays her eggs there and covers them with leaves. As the leaves rot, they heat up, keeping the eggs nice and warm – it's like built-in central heating. The mother can adjust the heating by piling up more leaves or scraping some away.

Inside the eggs the baby crocodiles are slowly growing. When they're nearly ready to hatch, they start chirping away like so many tiny birds. That's a signal for the mother to open up the nest.

Then, very very carefully, she
picks up the newly hatched
babies in her enormous
jaws and drops them in
the water nearby.

It takes 80-90 days for the eggs to be ready to hatch.

She still doesn't leave the babies to it, though.

She stands guard over them in the water for weeks and weeks.

You see, lots of things like to eat baby crocodiles – birds like
storks and herons, snakes, big fish and, I'm sorry to say …

other crocodiles. Some of those other crocodiles living nearby are likely to be the baby crocodiles' relatives – their uncles and aunts or even...

Well, now you can probably work out what I meant about the fathers.

Despite the mother's best efforts, a lot of the babies
meet an unfortunate end.

But the ones that survive grow ...

and **grow** ...

It normally takes about two years for
a baby crocodile to grow to 1m and another eight
years or so for it
to reach 2m.

and **grow**.

Until one day, they're the ones lurking in the water by that spot
on the bank, with only their eyes and their noses sticking out ...

waiting for something – or even somebody – to come down to drink.

ABOUT CROCODILES

Crocodiles are reptiles like snakes, lizards and turtles. Their closest relatives are alligators and caimans. There are sixteen different kinds altogether. The ones in the story are saltwater crocodiles, the biggest of the lot – they can reach 6 or 7m in length. They are found in south and southeast Asia, Australia, New Guinea, Vanuatu and the Solomon Islands. They sometimes go out to sea, but usually live in big rivers and swamps. Crocodiles are also found in North, Central and South America, Africa and the Caribbean.

There are two kinds of alligator and six kinds of caiman. One species of alligator lives in China, where it's very rare; the other lives in North America. The caimans live in Central and South America. Both alligators and caimans look a lot like crocodiles – it can be quite hard to tell them apart. The easiest way is to look at their teeth when their mouths are shut (though don't get too close!). If you can see teeth sticking up at the side of the mouth, it's a crocodile – if you can't, it's an alligator or a caiman.

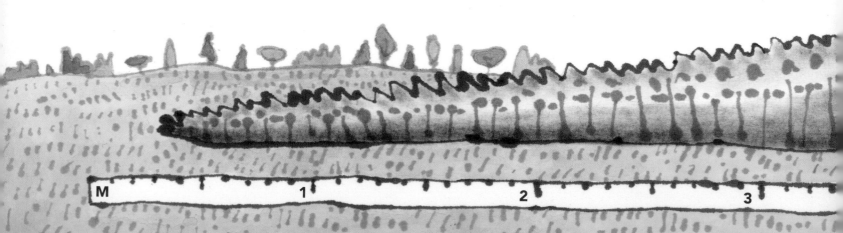

MORE INFORMATION

The best place to find out about crocodiles is **iucncsg.org**.

You can also find a lot of useful information at **crocodilian.com**.

INDEX

Look up the pages to find out about all these crocodile things. Don't forget to look at both kinds of word – **this kind** and **this kind.**

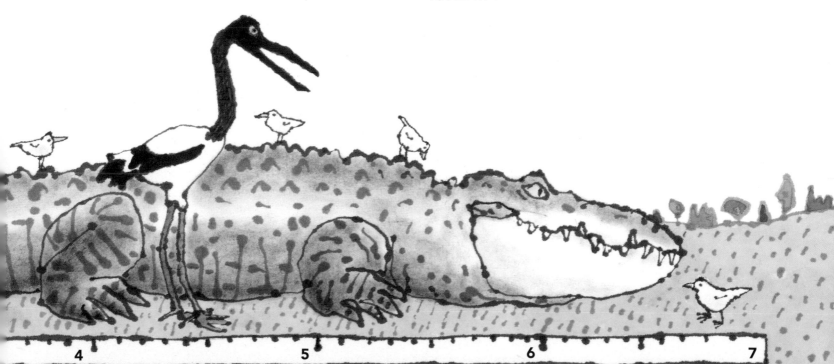

4   5   6   7

Note to Parents

Sharing books with children is one of the best ways to help them learn. And it's one of the best ways they learn to read, too.

Nature Storybooks are beautifully illustrated, award-winning information picture books whose focus on animals has a strong appeal for children. They can be read as stories, revisited and enjoyed again and again, inviting children to become excited about a subject, to think and discover, and to want to find out more.

Each book is an adventure into the real world that broadens children's experience and develops their curiosity and understanding – and that's the best kind of learning there is.

Note to Teachers

Nature Storybooks provide memorable reading experiences for children in Key Stages 1 and 2 (Years 1–4), and also offer many learning opportunities for exploring a topic through words and pictures.

By working with the stories, either individually or together, children can respond to the animal world through a variety of activities, including drawing and painting, role play, talking and writing.

The books provide a rich starting-point for further research and for developing children's knowledge of information genres.

Nature Storybooks support the literacy curriculum in a variety of ways, providing:

* a focus for a whole class topic
* high-quality texts for guided reading
* a resource for the class read-aloud programme
* information texts for the class and school library for developing children's individual reading interests

Find more information on how to use Nature Storybooks in the classroom at
www.walker.co.uk/naturestorybooks

Nature Storybooks support KS 1–2 English and KS 1–2 Science